Copyright © 2011 by Erin B. Larson 85261-LARS

ISBN: Softcover   978-1-4568-5216-0
       Hardcover   978-1-4568-5217-7

All rights reserved. No part of this book may be reproduced or transmitted in any form or by any means, electronic or mechanical, including photocopying, recording, or by any information storage and retrieval system, without permission in writing from the copyright owner.

This book was printed in the United States of America.

To order additional copies of this book, contact:
Xlibris Corporation
1-888-795-4274
www.Xlibris.com
Orders@Xlibris.com

Dedication

To my husband Josh, who lifts me up and keeps me grounded. To my daughters who make my heart smile and my world sweet, and to my Dad who inspired my love for all things creative.

Summertime is my favorite time of year. The trees have their leaves, the flowers are in bloom and the birds are singing their songs.

My little sister, Amy, helps Mommy and I plant the last of the flowers in the garden.

Mommy digs the holes and Amy and I put the flowers in.

Sometimes Amy forgets to plant her flowers and plays in the dirt instead. She's so silly!

Mommy says that it's good when it rains because it waters the flowers and makes everything grow. I just love the sound of it!

Amy and I love to put on our rain boots and jackets to play in the rain. Peyton really wants to go with us but she's too little to even walk!

Summertime at our house is soooo much fun!

We are always playing and doing fun things outside.

We love to eat ice cream with sprinkles...

...we find sand dollars and special shells on the beach.

Daddy takes us on boat rides. Amy and I sit on his lap and he even lets us drive!

We eat watermelon and corn on the cob...

...and Amy and I get to dance around and wave our flags.

After a long, fun filled day Daddy and Mommy tuck us in our beds for a good nights sleep

Then we wake up and do it again tomorrow!